What Food Chain?

by Heather Nicole

Contents

Harcourt

Orlando Boston Dallas Chicago San Diego

www.harcourtschool.com

Here are the plants that grow
by the pond.

Who eats the plants that grow by the pond?

The insect eats the plants.

Who eats the insect that eats the plants that grow by the pond?

The fish eats the insect.

Who eats the fish that eats the insect that eats the plants that grow by the pond?

The bird eats the fish.

Children eat fish, too!

A Food Chain

Index